The Life
of
Gus

D1367468

The Life of GUS

of

The Dog with the Big Head

Sandee Roquemore-Maxwell

ARCHWAY
PUBLISHING

Archway Publishing books may be ordered through booksellers or by contacting:

Archway Publishing
1663 Liberty Drive
Bloomington, IN 47403
www.archwaypublishing.com
1 (888) 242-5904

Because of the dynamic nature of the Internet, any web addresses or
links contained in this book may have changed since publication and
may no longer be valid. The views expressed in this work are solely those
of the author and do not necessarily reflect the views of the publisher,
and the publisher hereby disclaims any responsibility for them.

Any people depicted in stock imagery provided by Getty Images are
models, and such images are being used for illustrative purposes only.
Certain stock imagery © Getty Images.

This book is a work of non-fiction. Unless otherwise noted, the author
and the publisher make no explicit guarantees as to the accuracy of
the information contained in this book and in some cases, names of
people and places have been altered to protect their privacy.

ISBN: 978-1-4808-7419-0 (sc)
ISBN: 978-1-4808-7420-6 (e)

Library of Congress Control Number: 2019934404

Print information available on the last page.

Archway Publishing rev. date: 3/15/2019

This book is dedicated to Gus, Trixie and all the other street dogs in the world.

I also want to acknowledge Laura Forma, Rob Acuna, Jr and Tom Heller for their rescue of Gus; their never-ending love and energy for street animals is amazing.

This book is also dedicated to Anna Barbosa and the rest of the Houston K-911 Rescue group, without you, so many street dogs would die a slow and painful death.

I also want to send out a special thanks to all the thousands of people who donated and cared so much for Gus.

Plus, thank you to all the networkers and street rescuers who shed their blood, sweat and tears to save lives, you are true life savers.

Kudos to Steven C Smith for his patient assistance with my computer issues, you are a computer genius.

Lastly, none of this would be possible without the support of my family, especially my rescue "mentor", my daughter, Shelby Roquemore.

Chapter 1

Happy Days

Hi, my name is Gus, and this is the story of my life. You probably won't believe all that has happened to me, but I am going to tell you all about it. I haven't always been called Gus, when I was just a little guy, my boy named me Rex. My boy's name was Timmy and when I first went to live with him, I was happy. I thought my life would always be how it was right then. Timmy was so good to me. We were always together.

Timmy wanted to take me everywhere he went. We went on long walks through our neighborhood and sometimes he even took me to the park. Afterwards, he would give me a bath, brush my short, shiny coat a bit and then we would lay on his bed and drift off to sleep while he read me a story out loud.

The days were warm and sunny, and we played fetch together outside almost every day. I made Timmy so happy when he threw the ball and I brought it back to him. We spent countless hours doing this over and over again. He was so proud of me and I wanted nothing more than to please him.

You wouldn't believe how much I loved it when Timmy would roll me over and scratch my belly. It may sound silly, but my absolute favorite thing was when he looked into my eyes and told me I was a "good boy". I remember thinking that I was absolutely the luckiest dog in the whole world, but one day, things started to change.

I remember it like it was yesterday. One day Timmy sat me down and told me he had to go to a place called "school". He told me I would be all alone during the day and now I had to stay outdoors while they were all gone for the day.

But Timmy told me not to worry, he said he would come home right after school to play with me and we would spend every minute together once he was home. I admit it, I was worried, but I trusted Timmy to always take care of me so I tried to act brave so I would still be Timmy's "good boy".

At first things were ok. Timmy would run all the way home, dart through the house and bust out the back door in a flash. It seemed like he missed me as much as I missed him. I couldn't wait to hear his voice. The minute he arrived home, he would put his books down and come out back and yell, "Rex, come here boy!"

He would tell me how much he loved me and that he wished he could stay home all day like he did in the summer. We would often sit on the back porch and share our favorite after-school snack, a big red apple all sliced up by Timmy's mom.

Then we would play for a while before supper and settle down for the night to rest. I realized that being home alone all day was not fun at all, but I felt I could make this work and I vowed to never let Timmy know how much I missed him while he was gone.

Timmy was my whole world. He fed me, gave me fresh water to drink, he gave me all the love and attention that a dog like me would want. And in return, I adored Timmy. I just knew I would spend the rest of my life making Timmy proud, protecting him and loving him with my whole heart.

Chapter 2
School Brings Changes

As time passed, I saw less and less of Timmy. You see, he made new friends at school and he wanted to "play ball" with them after school instead of me. I still wanted to be Timmy's "good dog" so I tried my best to be happy being alone, but I missed him so very much.

One day I heard Timmy and his friend heading out to Ben's house to "play video games". I didn't know what a video game was, but I knew I loved to "play" anything. I figured Timmy had forgotten how much I loved to "play" so he didn't take me with him. But I could solve this problem.

I scratched and scratched at the side gate, I pushed with all my might, but the gate did not budge. That obviously wasn't working so I had to think of a new plan. Then it hit me, I would squeeze UNDER the gate. But I was a just a little too big so I began to dig and dig until I had moved enough dirt so I could squeeze my body out to the other side.

The only problem was, Timmy and Ben were gone now, they were nowhere to be found. I lifted my head high in the air trying to catch a whiff of my boy, but there was nothing! All I could smell was Mr. Carter cooking outside. It smelled like he was grilling hot dogs and hamburgers. Mr. Carter was our neighbor and he was outside almost as much as me, grilling and working in his garden.

So, what was I going to do now? I started sniffing the ground, however, all I could smell was old scents of Timmy going in both directions on our sidewalk, so which one should I pick? After searching up and down our block until I was hot and tired, I finally gave up and went to sit on our porch.

I figured Timmy would be sure to see me when he came home and he would know how much I wanted to spend time with him, so next time he would take me with him instead of leaving me home alone. I just knew that when he came home, I would surely get some of his special love once he realized I had been out searching for him, right?

But boy was I wrong. Timmy was so upset with me. He kept telling me I could have gotten lost or hit by a car. He immediately took me to the backyard and scolded me even more. He told me to "sit" and "stay" and I did exactly that.

My whole plan had not turned out the way I thought it would. A few minutes later I saw Timmy coming out the back door with something in his hand....... what was that? He sat down beside me and tied multiple long shoelaces together. Then he tied one end around a tree and the other end around my neck.

Oh boy, now I could no longer run along the fence or even chase squirrels. And it certainly wasn't long enough for me to sleep on our back porch any more. But I trusted Timmy, if he thought this was best, I would have to learn to "deal with it" like he told me to do as he headed back inside.

I was scared sleeping outside all alone. There were all kinds of noises that I did not recognize. This was new to me and I did not like it at all, but I really had no choice, this was my life. All I could do was HOPE for things to go back like they once were one day soon.

As time passed, I saw Timmy less and less. Some days the only time I saw him was when he ran outside to give me my bowl of food. I no longer got two meals a day and most of the time he forgot to give me fresh water too. Often when he came out, he would not even stop to pat my head.

But no matter what, I still loved Timmy with all my heart. He was my boy. I am sure he didn't know how much I missed him, how much I wanted to lay on his bed while he read me a story. How I longed for the days we spent playing ball and laying in the grass sharing a snack and just being together. If he had only known, I am sure he would have made more time for me, right?

I grew bigger and the days grew cooler. Some nights I was so cold that my teeth would chatter. Yes, even with my shiny brown and gold fur I was still as "cold as ice". My whole body would shake and shiver and there was nothing I could do to stop it. And speaking of ice, sometimes it was even so cold that the water in my bowl would freeze solid like a big chunk of ice and I could no longer even get a drink.

I guess it must have been too cold for Timmy to come outside because many days he didn't even come out to feed me. The only thing worse than being outside in the cold is being outside in the cold and being HUNGRY TOO. Believe me, you don't want to have to live like that. And when it rained, my life went from bad to worse, I was cold, wet and hungry. Can you imagine how I felt? Some days I felt so weak that I thought I could not make it even one more day.

As I spent all those cold, lonely days and nights, I had lots of time to think. I could not understand why my life was so very different now. I still loved Timmy and surely, he still loved me too, right? I remembered that I had gotten out of the back yard once, and I sometimes got bored now that I was home alone and I had dug a few holes, but surely that was not enough to make Timmy stop loving me, right?

Timmy was still ALL I had in the whole world and I loved him the same as I always had. I just could not imagine what I had done to cause all these changes. I had to believe that one day school would be over, and Timmy would spend his time at home playing with me all day once again. That's all that I could hang on to, that's all that kept me from giving up.

Chapter 3

The Move

I was so happy when the weather turned a little warmer. The grass was growing again, and I heard talk through the back door that school was almost over. I wish I wasn't still tied up, I wanted so badly to get close to the door to hear everything that was being said.

My heart just about jumped out of my chest when I thought about my life being like it was before Timmy went to school. This was what I had been waiting for, what I had been dreaming of. Timmy would be all mine again. I could hardly stand my excitement. And just when I thought it was all going to be good again, I found out how very wrong I was.

School was finally over, and instead of this being the best day ever, something REALLY BAD happened. Something I am ashamed to tell you. Timmy and his family put all their things in a huge truck with a box on the back. Then they all got in the car and drove away......I stood there confused, wondering what was happening. I could not believe my eyes.

I was sure they just forgot me. I was certain that any minute now they would realize what they had done, and Timmy would come running back to untie me and take me with him. But days passed and no one came......

I became so hungry and sad. I knew I needed to be Timmy's good boy, so I had to wait right here. That way when he came back, I would be exactly where he left me. But I also knew I was so very hungry. I had no idea what I could do, but I knew I needed to do SOMETHING.

I was becoming weaker by the day and I had already drunk all of the rainwater in my bowl too. I decided there was nothing left for me to do other than to chew on my string until I was free. Then I knew I had to quickly go find food and water. I decided that after I was refreshed, I would hurry back to our yard. I just HAD to be waiting here when Timmy came back. I just knew he was somewhere out there missing me as much as I missed him.

It actually wasn't too hard once I decided to chew on the string to get free, I had known all along I could break the string free from the tree. But Timmy wanted me to stay here and I wanted to please him, so that is what I had tried to do.

Once I was free, I headed over to the fence. Getting under the gate was a little harder because I was more grown up now, but I dug a bit more and quickly got to the other side. So, there I was, once again I was out of my yard, out in the big scary world. Now what?

I knew I had a lot to learn. I knew I needed to work fast to find something to eat and drink and thankfully I didn't have to go far. Timmy had always told me that I had a good snout. Once he told me that I could smell things a hundred times better than he could and now it was time for me to put my snout to the test.

Now where was that smell coming from? It smelled sweet but spicy and I soon discovered it was coming from the big can beside Mr. Carter's house. But I still had one problem, how could I get what was inside that big thing out here so I could eat it? I knew I could not lift up the lid and stick my head inside- I was way too short, that was never going to work.

It seemed the only way I could do it was to use my body to push the whole thing over. It took me a great deal of work, but it finally toppled over with a thud. I could hardly believe my luck.

Boy was I surprised, there were no bags of dog food to gobble down, but there were all sorts of scraps of food and I ate until I couldn't hold another bite. I devoured greasy French fries, beans, scraps of bread and stale chocolate cake like what I had seen when Timmy turned 10.

I was so hungry, and it felt good doing down. I ate all I could hold and then I went back to my yard and laid down "like a good dog". I was so happy to be back in my yard, back where Timmy could find me.

However, it did not take too long before I wasn't feeling so good anymore. My tummy hurt so bad, I knew I had to give some of what I had eaten back to Mr. Carter. So, I ran back next door and immediately returned most of what I had gobbled down, and I hoped Mr. Carter would forgive me for stealing food from his big metal can.

Maybe my body was upset because I had taken food without permission? Or maybe I ate too much? Maybe I ate too fast? Whatever the cause, I felt horrible and I did not want to ever eat trash again if I could help it.

Chapter 4

Life on My Own

So, my days passed slowly. At first, I only left to find food or a puddle of water and then I would head right back to my yard crawling under my fence each time I came and went. I was so scared I would miss Timmy when he came back to get me. I was so very lonely, but I still held out hope that Timmy would return any day now.

I don't know how many days passed, and truly I would have stayed there forever, waiting on Timmy, but one day a new family moved in. I am sure it was a mistake, they just didn't realize it was MY house, right? Soon a lady came out back with a broom, I had seen these before, being pushed around on the floor by Timmy's mom, but this lady used it differently. She hit my behind with it and yelled "Get, get out of here, go home".

I had no other choice, I had to go. But didn't she understand, this WAS my home? How in the world was Timmy ever
going to be able to find me when he realized I was missing? I
decided there was nothing else I could do, I was going to have
to find Timmy myself. So, for days and days I walked around,
searching everywhere I could think of.

As I walked around hoping to find my beloved Timmy,
I also scrounged around for food, and I vowed to never give
up my search for my boy. At first, it was hard not to eat

EVERYTHING I found. But with time, I learned to never eat chocolate cake again. In fact, I learned that eating anything chocolate could make me deathly ill so I swore I would never eat that again, no matter how hungry I became.

I realized once again I had much to learn. I was so very lonely for a long time. And then one day, I saw a small scruffy dog. The dog smelled like a girl if my snout was right. But I decided that was OK, I knew I needed a friend and a girl would probably make a fine friend, right? However, when I tried to approach her, she immediately ran away.

Why would she be afraid of me? I knew I had grown to be pretty big, but I also knew I was a nice guy. How can I make her understand that I just wanted to be her friend? I spent my next few days looking for the scruffy dog. Every time I saw her and tried to get close to her, she would run off. But I didn't give up. I was determined to make her my first dog friend.

Then it happened. One day I heard some boys laughing and I also heard what sounded like a dog whimpering in fear and in pain. I rushed towards the sounds and I saw three boys. They were throwing rocks at my soon to be scruffy friend.

I don't know what came over me, but before I knew it, I had jumped between her and the boys and I was growling and showing my teeth. I had never done anything like this before. But something deep inside me knew I had to DO SOMETHING FAST before it was too late.

I must have been a sight because the three boys suddenly stopped and took off running in the other direction. I turned and looked at the little scruffy girl. She was hurt for sure, but she was no longer scared. She had limped over to me and nudged me with her nose, telling me "thank you" for what I had done.

She told me her name was Trixie and she was so glad I came to the rescue, she said I saved her life. I told her my name was Rex and she said that name sounded tough. I didn't tell her right then, but I didn't feel very tough. As a matter of fact, I think she saved me too.

Before Trixie, I felt like I was about to die from loneliness. Is it possible to die of loneliness? I really don't know, but I do know that now I finally had a glimmer of hope that maybe things might start getting better for me.

Chapter 5

Friends

Trixie and I became fast friends and before I knew it, we were almost always together. We spent time searching for food, trying to find water to drink and looking for shelter when it rained. Life was hard, but it was much easier once I had a friend. My relationship with Trixie was not like my love for Timmy, but it was pretty darn close. Before we knew it, we were inseparable.

My body was getting bigger, I knew I was growing but my body was no longer muscular, and my fur was no longer thick and beautiful. Even though we spent most of the day looking for food, I was getting thinner and thinner. I tried to be sure Trixie had enough to eat, even if it meant I went hungry, and it was starting to show. I was no longer the beautiful dog I had once been.

I was so happy to have Trixie that winter. As the days grew colder, Trixie and I searched for a place to call our own. We found some old abandoned apartments and decided this was it, this was going to be our new home.

And believe me when I tell you that I was sure glad we found a place with a roof. At least this winter, I would not be out in the cold without shelter like I had been last year. It was not comfortable like Timmy's bed, but it was sure better than sleeping in the cold, wet mud.

It wasn't long before we woke up one morning with white stuff all over the ground. Neither of us had ever seen anything like it but we were both certain we would have died that winter had we not had each other for warmth, and an enclosed place to stay out of the cold. And although I really missed snuggling up in the bed with Timmy, I knew I had to make the best of my current situation.

Chapter 6

Growing Up

At first, I hardly remembered that I had anything around my neck. It had been there so long I truly forgot about it for a while. But the more time that passed, the more I realized something just wasn't right. It was almost like this thing around my neck was getting smaller by the day. Was that even possible?

I told Trixie about my concerns and she did her best to break it with her teeth, but she didn't really have good teeth. Sweet little Trixie, she was a bit of a mess. She would have done anything she could for me, and I felt the same way about her, but try as she might, she could NOT break the string around my neck so I figured I would just have to live with it. I figured maybe if I got big enough, it would just break on its own, right?

With every passing day, it seemed that my head was getting bigger, but Trixie didn't care, she still loved me just like I was.

And you know, Trixie's fur was a bit greasy, probably because before I came along, she hid under cars and trucks for safety, but she was absolutely beautiful to me. And sure, our little house was full of junk no one wanted, but it was ours. There were bars on the door to keep out any large intruders and we felt safe there.

So, we continued to try to make the best of our situation. We were grateful for each other. We would sometimes tell each other stories about our life before we met. She could hardly believe when I told her how much fun Timmy and I had playing together. I told her about sitting on the porch sharing an apple in the afternoon, the joy of tummy rubs and listening to Timmy read at night.

She told me about her life before she was a "street dog". She did NOT have a boy, she had a lady named Gloria who said she "adored" her. Trixie would go to a place called a groomer at least once a month and she left there smelling like a flower.

Trixie wasn't crazy about the smell, but Gloria seemed to like it, so Trixie said she did not complain. Trixie said she had a sweater for the winter and even a raincoat for when it rained. And she had all sorts of squeaky toys and even a nice pink collar.

Trixie told me that Gloria started feeling really bad one day and she was rushed away, and she never came back. That was the last time Trixie saw Gloria. After a few days, a stranger came to try to catch Trixie, but she said she became afraid, so she ran out the front door and never looked back.

We both missed our old lives, but we were sure happy we had found each other. Both good times and hard times are so much better with friends. And it was good to have someone we could rely on when things got tough. However, we both thought it might be nice to have a human friend again so that became our new mission. We would find a human together.

Chapter 7

Trouble Finds Me

The days were getting warmer again and I think school must have been out because suddenly there were more kids around. I actually love kids, well, all kids except those three that had been trying to hurt Trixie. I hoped we would never see those three again. So, as Trixie and I walked around looking in trash cans for food, we started searching for kids too.

Surely there were some nice kids close by, right? Each day we would scope out the area. One day we found what looked like some that would possibly be good to meet, but we didn't want to scare them off, so we knew we had to move slowly. Each day we would get a little closer, and we were sure to have a friendly tail wag the whole time.

One day, we thought we were making progress. The boys we had been watching every day were smiling and I could hear a few of them laughing too. They were trying to offer us treats. We thought this must be our lucky day. Maybe tonight we would have a new boy to call our very own.

Since Trixie was more timid than me, I decided I would walk up very slowly and retrieve the treat. figured I could bring it back to Trixie for us to share. But this turned out to be a really bad idea.

The bigger boy pulled out something that looked like a long stick and pointed it in my direction. All of a sudden, I started seeing little bead-like things coming out of the stick and immediately I started hurting all over my body. These little beads stung when they hit me, and I realized I was bleeding a little wherever I was hit.

We quickly retreated to the safety of our home, but not before I had been hit all over my body. Why did they do that? Were they afraid of me? I had been doing my best to look friendly. I just didn't understand. Didn't they know that we wanted to be their friend?

Trixie did her best to clean my wounds. She worked for hours trying to make me feel better. And then she searched for food on her own even though she was typically afraid to leave the house without me. She knew I was too injured to go with her today.

Trixie got lucky that first day out on her own. She brought me back a half-eaten piece of steak with a bone. I was so happy to get that steak and I could not wait to finish the meal off with that yummy bone, but Trixie warned me about bones. She said her mom had gotten very sick after eating a bone and Trixie was certain the two were related. She asked me to promise to never eat or chew on a bone and I gave her my word.

Chapter 8

Life is Hard

It was a very hot summer. When it went for days without raining it became hard to find fresh water. We both knew we HAD to have water, so even though I was still weak, and Trixie was going out alone getting our food, I still had to leave our home a few times a day to find water.

We often had to drink water from the side of the road or the ditch, but every time we did, we regretted it, we would be sick for days. But what were we to do? We needed water and we knew it. We must have water to stay alive.

After the incident with the kids and the long stick, we decided to be even more careful about who we trusted. There were some men who looked like they were building something close by and they sometimes offered us leftover pieces of burritos or sandwiches. But we were too afraid to go up and get them until the men had left for the day. We did not want to take any chances.

We were so grateful for these scraps. I was still becoming more and more weak every day, so it was hard for me to walk and my head was beginning to hurt. I could barely search for food at all and even when we found it, I had a hard time swallowing it.

Somehow deep inside me I knew something was wrong. There were times when it seemed hard to even breathe and my neck was becoming sore too. I had always tried to be positive and not to think about bad things, but I was REALLY starting to get worried.

Chapter 9
Can I Trust Again?

Finally, one day I knew I needed help. Trixie was out looking for food and I decided I must find someone to help me. I had always been afraid of the road. Last winter we saw another stray named Charlie get hit when he tried crossing the street chasing a squirrel, so both Trixie and I typically stayed away from the road. However, I knew that is where most of the people were so that is exactly where I went. Who knows, maybe Timmy and his family might drive by and see me, and then everything would be great again.

I never saw Timmy that morning, but I did see lots of cars and trucks. Most of them honked and yelled at me. All the people were acting odd, they were staring and calling me names. But this one car drove by slowly and a little girl inside saw me and started watching my every move, she rolled down her window and yelled at me to "stop".

Well I had learned my lesson. I was immediately afraid once I saw something in her hand. Maybe some little sharp things were going to start flying out of it and hit me like what happened with that long stick? I was so afraid that I quickly stopped my search for help, and I decided to run back to the safety of our own place before something bad happened to me again.

I hobbled back home and laid down on the cold hard floor to wait for Trixie. I knew I would have to tell her about my desperate search for help, but I had not told Trixie how bad I had been feeling. I did not want to worry her. She had no idea I was having difficulty swallowing and I definitely did not tell her it was getting harder to breathe.

Once Trix was home, that's what I called her sometimes, I told her all about my search and the girl who had wanted me to stop, but I didn't stop because I was afraid of the odd thing she had in her hand. She told me not to worry because no one had ever found our home so far and she was sure the little girl could not find me here.

We had no idea that the little girl had told all of her friends about me. Nor did we know that what she held in her hand was a phone with a camera and she had taken a picture of me to show everyone how bad I looked. Very soon, the little girl and all of her friends were searching everywhere trying to find me. And we certainly had no idea what was up ahead. Little did I know, but that day would change my life FOREVER.

The day passed and evening was coming so Trixie left again to find food. She knew I was way too sick to help her, so I stayed home alone. A little time had passed, and I started hearing voices. It sounded like two boys and a girl and I immediately became deathly afraid.

What if they threw cans at me? This had happened once before, and it was scary. I became soaked with what was coming out of the cans. Or they might throw rocks at me like those boys were doing to Trixie when I first met her. Or what if they had one of those long things that made me hurt all over when they pointed it my way? I was afraid but I was too sick and weak to run, so I just stayed where I was and hoped they would not find me.

Then, I heard the voices come closer. These kids sounded nice, but how could I be sure? They were not laughing and joking like the other kids had done. I don't know why, but for some reason I just knew they were not mean and that I could trust them. And I knew I needed them, I knew I needed help or surely I would no longer be around to protect Trixie. So, I stood up and walked around the corner and there they were.

The girl had that thing in her hand again but now instead of being afraid, I was hopeful. Hopeful that they would help me. I heard one of the boys say that they should always get an adult before approaching a stray dog.

Then the girl ran off. I immediately thought I might have scared her, or maybe I looked too bad and she could not bear to see my any longer. I was a bit confused but there was nothing else for me to do other than wait to see what happened next.

Chapter 10
No Other Options

Even though the boys did not seem afraid of me, they did not come close to me. They just waited patiently at the metal gate that was the door to our house. But something odd was happening, they had water in their eyes. This was the first time I had ever seen such a thing in my life, and I had no idea what it meant. Their faces did not look mean or angry, their eyes looked sad and they kept talking to me through the gate in soft and gentle tones.

I wasn't sure what was going to happen next, but I just knew I could trust them. Then the girl came back with her mom and a big metal thing that they placed on the ground. I was not sure exactly what they wanted me to do but it looked like they wanted me to get in, so I slowly and carefully walked over and went inside. The boys quickly shut the gate on the metal box and picked it up with me inside. Then they took me to a car.

I had been in a car once, a long time ago when I was a young puppy. I was scared that time and I was a little scared this time too, but I was also tired and weak, so I just laid down and let them take me wherever they wanted. I didn't have the strength to do anything else. I will tell you the truth, I was a bit concerned about what was up ahead for me, but really, my biggest concern was for Trixie. She would be scared and all alone and she would never know what had happened to me.

Maybe she would think I had just run off and left her all alone? I sure hope not. I hope she would always know how much I loved her, and I promised myself that one day when I was feeling better, I would do my best to find her again. But for now, all I could do was sleep.

When I awoke, we had arrived at a place where there were a lot of other dogs and even some cats too. I could not see them, but I could smell them. They immediately put me in a room and lots of people circled around me.

They sat me up on a big metal thing so I was up very high. I was right up close to them and they were all staring at me. But no one laughed. No one hit me or threw things at me, and even though I had no idea where I was, I knew I had to trust them.

This person who seemed to be in charge started by looking at me from my nose to my tail. They decided that I was in pain and boy were they right. They told me they were going to do their best to help me and I believed them. Then they said they were going to give me something for pain and immediately I went back into a deep sleep.

I dreamed about playing fetch with Timmy, then we went inside and got on Timmy's bed to rest. I dreamed about when I was little, and in my dream, I had fresh water and food every day. I remembered the joy of a good belly rub. It felt like things were as they once had been so long ago.... until I WOKE UP!

Now I could definitely breathe better, but I immediately realized I was not home with Timmy. I was far from home and once again I had no idea what was happening. All sorts of people were working on me and they were calling me Gus.

I tried to tell them that my name was Rex, but they didn't seem to understand me. And to tell you the truth, I liked the name Gus, and I figured I was not the little puppy that I once was. I was no longer carefree and full of hope, so I figured a new name was probably a good idea.

I took a lot of naps those days, and each time I woke up, I realized I felt a little bit better. I stayed there for a little while, and then for some reason, they put me back in the car and we took a long road trip. I arrived at another place and there were even more people.

I heard that this was a school so at first, I was afraid. Once Timmy went to school, he no longer had time for me. But for some reason, the people in this school had plenty of time for me. Still, every day I was feeling a little better than I had the day before, and I was really glad all these people seemed to know exactly what I needed.

Chapter 11

A Star is Born

Those days were amazingly odd. People brought me treats and toys. I had not had toys in a really long time, and I did not remember what to do with them at first. But it all started coming back and I was so happy. They told me that people from all sorts of places cared about me. They told me that everyone was "rooting" for me and even though I had no idea what that meant, it sure sounded good.

They told me that people all around the world had heard my story and they wanted to help me. I had no idea how big the world was, but it sure sounded grand. I heard them say that my story was on TV and on the Internet. I didn't even know what either of those things were, but from the sound of their voice, that was a very good thing.

I have no idea how long I stayed at the school, but they took great care of me. One day they said I could go stay at a "foster home" and I wasn't sure what that meant either, but I believed that these people would only do what was best for me, so I was OK with it.

I continued to get stronger every day and my foster mom took me back to the school for visits all the time. They did all these things called "treatments" on me and even though they weren't really what I had known as a "treat", it did seem to help so I never complained. They would put these odd glasses on my eyes and then they rubbed a wand around on my neck and it did seem to help.

And you won't believe it! The little girl and the two boys who saved me came to see me at my foster home. I found out that the girl was named Laura and the boys were named Rob and Tom. They seemed so happy to see me and I was happy to see them too, I remembered that they saved my life and I wanted to thank them. I gave them all kisses, and they rubbed my tummy and scratched behind my ears just the way I love it!

Everyone that came to visit me told me that I would never have to worry about food again, and that I would always have my own bed. This sounded heavenly but seeing Laura, Rob and Tom again made me think about Trixie.

How was she doing? Was she safe? Did she make friends with any of the other street dogs in our neighborhood? I did hope she was not alone. She was too small to live alone, and I was so afraid I would never see her again.

Chapter 12

Second Chances

Then one day they said I was well enough to go home for good. But where is home? Were they going to take me back to the building Trixie and I shared? I was once again confused but by now I had truly learned to trust these people. A lady named Anna came to get me. She told me that she would be my momma now and she told me she was taking me home to meet my new brother. She also told me that she had a BIG surprise for me.

As we drove back to Houston my mind was mostly full of happy memories. I was glad to be the dog named "Gus". And I had no idea what "a star" was but I knew I enjoyed being one. But of course, I was sad when I thought about my Trix though, I tried not to worry about my friend, but I loved her and really hoped she was ok.

You won't believe what happened next. I have never been so shocked and amazed in all my life. When we got to Momma Anna's house, guess what I saw?

My sweet Trixie was there! But something was very different about her. She was clean and no longer skinny. She looked so sure of herself too, she was no longer scared of people. She had evidently been eating good and her fur was beautiful. She had on a shiny new collar, nothing like that shoe string I had around my neck for so long. She looked so happy, and that made my day.

I later found out that Laura and her friends had gone back looking for my buddies and they found Trixie. She was staying with a "foster", but someone was interested in adopting her so she would have a new home soon.

How had they known about Trixie? Maybe they heard me talk about her in my dreams? Or maybe they saw her that day while looking for me? I wasn't sure, but all I knew was that my life was once again perfect. Trixie and I were being treated like royalty.

Well, you probably won't believe it, but Trixie and I both have a home now and we both live INSIDE again. We don't live together, but we do still see each other. We get fed twice a day, we have fresh water, and we even get to go on walks EVERY DAY! Can you believe our luck?

Sometimes Laura, Rob and Tom come to get us and take us for what I learned is called a "car ride". I never knew how fun those could be. Sometimes they take us to get treats, and sometimes they take us for a "puppuccino", boy do I love those!

Some days we go out so I can meet people. They say I am an "example" and that my story will help dogs out there who are just like we were not so long ago. They even had a parade for me, and we walked through the park making people aware of what they call the "stray crisis" in Houston.

I don't understand all of that, but what I do know is how

much I love all of these people. I want them to know that they saved my life, and I would do anything for them.

I do hope my story helps all of the other dogs out in Houston and all of the other places in the world where dogs are not being treated with love and respect. Laura, Rob and Tom saved me because they saw me in pain and knew I needed help. I sure hope there are more kids out there like these three.

So, if you see any of my buddies, will you go get an adult and then do what you can to help them? And please be on the lookout for animals being mistreated too. Momma Anna says every dog deserves to be treated like we are being treated now.

I would really appreciate it if you would help us save animals in need. Please tell everyone one you know that there are thousands of animals just like me who need their help. And if you ever see Timmy, tell him I still love him, but I am safe and happy now. I am in good hands with people who love me.

Thanks for listening to my story. Maybe I can tell you about other adventures in my life soon, I would really like that.

Love,
Gus

Houston K 911 Rescue- from left to right- Anna Barbosa,
Michelle Haberland, Kelly Halker, and Gus the dog in front.

The story of Gus is based on a true story. The reality is many people probably saw Gus before Laura did, but no one else took the time and initiative to do anything about his condition.

Thousands of animals just in the Houston area alone are suffering and they need us to step up and help. Many places in the United States, and other countries too, have the same type of animal crisis.

We do hope that each of you reading this story will decide right now to do something when you come across an animal in need. They are relying on US to do the right thing.

Remember, never approach an animal that is not familiar to you alone. ALWAYS get an adult to come and help. Animals who are sick or injured can sometimes be afraid, and it is easy for you to get bit or injured in other ways, so you need an adult that you can trust to take the lead until everyone is certain it is safe.

If you SEE SOMETHING, SAY SOMETHING and most importantly, DO SOMETHING!

Gus in Aug 2018 when he was first rescued off the street.

Gus was a street dog in Houston picked up Aug 29, 2018 by Laura Forma, Rob Acuna, Jr and Tom Heller. He was immediately rushed to the emergency room because he was in poor condition. He had been shot repeatedly with a pellet gun and he had these embedded all over this body. He also had a shoe lace tied around his neck causing his head to swell 3-4 x the normal size. This was making it hard for him to eat or drink and it was even impeding his airway.

Anna Barbosa and her rescue group, Houston K-911, immediately agreed to sponsor Gus. He was stabilized and transferred to Texas A&M School of Veterinary Medicine where he stayed for several weeks.

Gus became an Internet sensation and news of his past and his treatment spread across the globe. People donated money and followed his story and still do today. He truly has become the face of the "Street Dog Crisis" in Houston where it has been estimated there are over 1 million strays.

If you would like to learn more about this rescue group, you can go to Facebook and look for Houston K-911 Rescue or go to their website at houstonk911rescue.org. Rescue groups survive and save animals from the donations they receive, so feel free to be a part of saving lives by donating directly to this group.

If you want to learn more about how to help other strays like Gus, you can search on Facebook at Citizens for Houston's Strays. This is a group dedicated to helping the street dogs of Houston and surrounding areas.

Please be sure to follow Gus on his very own Facebook page, Gus' Journey. You can get updates about Gus, order a Gus T-shirt or hoodie, and meet all of Gus' new friends.

From left to right- Laura Forma, Tom Heller, Anna Barbosa, Rob Acuna, Jr, Brenda Carrizales and Gus the dog in front.

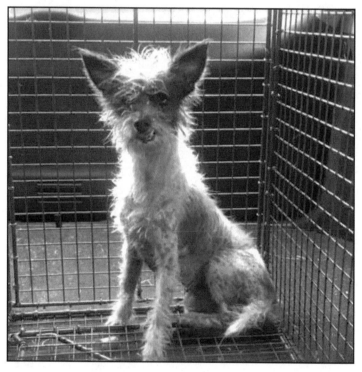

Trixie in Aug 2018 when she was first rescued off the street.

Printed and bound by PG in the USA